A PORTRAIT OF JACO

THE SOLOS COLLECTION

by Sean Malone

ISBN 978-0-634-01754-4

HAL•LEONARD® CORPORATION
7777 W. BLUEMOUND RD. P.O. BOX 13819 MILWAUKEE, WI 53213

A PORTRAIT OF JACO
THE SOLOS COLLECTION

CONTENTS

INTRODUCTION

"I ain't just wigglin' my fingers...
This is the real deal!"

Few people in the history of music have single-handedly transformed the way an instrument is played; virtuosi are strewn across centuries, and tales of their superhuman performances stir our imagination. Fewer still are performers who create a manner of playing so original that it forces us to see the instrument anew. With technique that exceeded the limits of physical endurance and musicality that attained oceanic depths, Jaco Pastorius created a style of playing that reinvented the electric bass. This is not to say that others haven't advanced the instrument and contributed to its evolution, it's just that Jaco started a *revolution*.

"Where I come from,
nobody cares what style of music you play.
Everybody down there just lives."

Born into a musical family, Jaco was exposed to music from the day he was born. Gifted with absolute pitch and immense hands, Jaco's musical future seemed inevitable. He lacked a formal music education, instead Jaco was bombarded by the rich cultural climate Florida had to offer, void of any musical prejudices. This allowed him to develop his own unique approach to music and the bass guitar without being pressured to play any *one* kind of music. He began to develop an underground reputation during his teen years while honing his playing technique, gigging regionally, and paying his dues. By the time he released his début LP and joined Weather Report, the Pastorius revolution garnered a worldwide audience, and Jaco quickly ascended to the self-ordained rank of "World's Greatest Bassist."

Despite the fact that most of us, including myself, never met Jaco, it's interesting how we almost always refer to him as 'Jaco'—as if he's been a lifelong friend of ours. In some ways, he has. Anyone who has had such a tremendous impact on our lives as musicians becomes something much more than just a collection of CDs, pictures, and videos; he becomes part of that indescribable transcendence we experience while listening to and playing music. Anyone who shares or contributes to this sense of wonder inevitably becomes a part of it.

"All you've got to do is keep your ears open.
Most of my musical knowledge comes from
playing experience."

We are on the cusp of the first generation of bassists born after Jaco's untimely death in 1987, so it's only appropriate that a series of books documenting Jaco's work are finally beginning to appear. This book chronicles Jaco's improvisational development, and as we'll see, many of the concepts utilized in his first few recordings serve as a model for the rest of his recorded output. By taking a closer look at these concepts, we may better understand Jaco's musical mind and discover why his playing was so revolutionary. To accommodate this, each transcription is accompanied by a brief analysis that discusses salient structural features.

In slow motion, we can dissect, divide, and combine every characteristic of Jaco's musical language, except the most important: the intangible, ineffable, larger-than-life aura that surrounded him and everything he did. In other words, you can't separate the music from the man. But the music he has left us reveals the most intimate details of his musical genius, transporting us directly to the moment of their creation, providing intimate contact with his astonishing musicianship and creativity.

The excerpts in this book span the entirety of Jaco's "official" recording career (those recordings he knew were going to be released), including landmark solos from his 1976 solo début, through Weather Report, to the Brian Melvin Trio. The transcriptions portray Jaco as a multifaceted performer and composer, drawing on influences ranging from Jimi Hendrix to Igor Stravinsky, manifested in purring fretless melodies to feedback-driven harmonics. The inclusion of tablature in this collection serves only as a point of reference; it is impossible to say with any certainty which fingering Jaco used when playing these pieces. However, extensive video documentation—including his instructional video, and concerts with Joni Mitchell, the Word of Mouth Band, and Weather Report—were utilized to coordinate fingering in specific cases.

By studying, discussing, and performing Jaco's music, we help to ensure the preservation of his legacy. Because of this one person, many bassists today—even those in their teens—are ripping through *Donna Lee*, playing lightning-fast solos, glittering harmonics, and deep, fingerstyle funk grooves; each time they do, they whisper a silent "thank you" to Jaco Pastorius.

Sean Malone
Eugene, Oregon
September 2001

DONNA LEE

By Charlie Parker

The first track from Jaco's 1976 début solo CD, *Jaco Pastorius*, was the "track heard 'round the world." Jaco chose the bebop classic *Donna Lee* in duet with percussionist Don Alias. Despite the claim made by Miles Davis that he, rather than Charlie Parker, composed this tune, there is no conclusive proof; however, there is some anecdotal evidence that supports this claim. In the late 1940s, Gil Evans was planning to make an arrangement of the tune and approached Davis for the music. Also, a common reason for recording alternate takes during Davis' time with Charlie Parker was because of missed notes on Davis' part. However, this was not the case when *Donna Lee* was recorded, which either indicates that Davis spent some extra time on it, or supports the notion that he composed it. Nonetheless, history has favored Charlie Parker as the composer.

As if performing the finger-twisting melody on bass was not enough, Jaco proceeds to solo through three choruses of the form. No one had dared to play music such as this on electric bass, much less with such astonishing musicality. Jaco's producer, Bobby Colomby, indicated that the track was finished in one or two takes, which suggests Jaco had most—if not all—of his solo worked out beforehand.

Donna Lee has a 32-bar form based on the changes to *Back Home Again in Indiana*. After the statement of the tune, Jaco arpeggiates an A♭ major triad, leading into his first solo chorus. In measures 35 and 36, Jaco substitutes an E7♯9 over the B♭7 chord with an open E string and harmonics for the notes G♯, D, and G. Soon afterward, he spans almost the entire bass neck with a whole-half diminished scale based on B♭, then substitutes D7 over the A♭ harmony in measure 40—a tritone substitution he frequently used.

Measure 47 contains the first occurrence of what would become a Pastorius trademark: eighth-note triplets in four-note groups, outlining descending seventh-chord arpeggios. The effect is polyrhythmic—the feeling of two separate pulses within the bar that don't share an equal division. It feels as if something is slowing down (the harmonic rhythm) and at the same time, something is speeding up (the eighth-note triplets are faster than the regular eighths.) As we will see, Jaco utilizes this same technique (including groupings of five) in many of his solos.

Jaco begins the second chorus in measure 65 with a phrase that resembles the original melody and ends it by emphasizing the upper extensions of the B♭7 chord: A♭, C, E♭, and G. Though the rhythmic drive remains consistent, this chorus has a more "searching" quality to it and contains shorter, more compact statements. Jaco extends the E♭7 chord in measures 79–80, adding the ♯9th, clustered in a group of harmonics that includes the major 7th, minor 7th, and major 3rd of the chord.

The final chorus is a statement of the melody in E major, prepared by a series of ii–V–I progressions. Jaco starts off with a pattern consisting of an arpeggiated minor seventh chord beginning with the 5th on the downbeats, approached by a ♭9 and ♯9. Beat three always has the 3rd of the dominant seventh, followed by the ♯9. This modulating sequence yields underlying stepwise motion that gives the impression of a compound melody—two melodic lines in one.

If everything were spelled in a theoretically strict way, the sequence would end up resolving to the chord F♭. However, in order to make things more readable, I switched to G♯m7 instead of A♭m7, setting up a iii–VI–ii–V–I progression in E.

At the point where G#m7 occurs, Jaco breaks the pattern. If he had continued the sequence, it would have looked like this:

This would have maintained the continuous stepwise descent on beats 1 and 3. The slight change Jaco made adds variety to a line that, despite the inclusion of colorful altered tones, would sound like a predictable sequence. Finally, the stylized statement of the tune in E major climaxes with an extended chromatic run, ending with a harmonic-laden E6/9 chord.

Jaco's performance of *Donna Lee* reveals each of the melodic, rhythmic, and harmonic devices that we will see in all of his recorded output. These devices include rhythmic displacement (triplets in groupings of four and five), arpeggios of seventh chords connected by step, harmonics to bolster the harmony, highly accurate rhythmic phrasing, utilization of the entire bass neck, double stops, emphasis of upper extensions (9ths, 11ths, and 13ths), and graceful melodicism. With this one track, Jaco Pastorius single-handedly forced us to see the bass guitar in a new light and created a new standard for the *virtuoso* bassist.

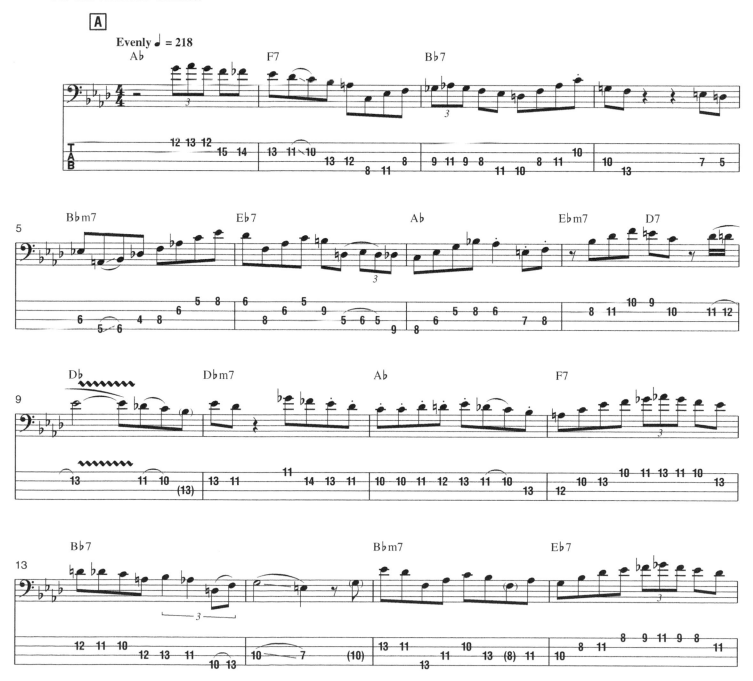

CONTINUUM

By Jaco Pastorius

For most of the selections in this book, Jaco is soloing as a sideman in the context of someone else's composition, within a group setting. In the case of "Continuum," we have the best of all possible worlds: Jaco is the composer, the piece is written essentially for solo bass, and he is the only soloist. The deep, rich, chorused tones come from double-tracking his bass, reportedly finished in two takes. The compositional contour is straightforward and traditional: 1) Statement of the melody, presenting the form and harmonic content; 2) Improvisation over the form that gradually builds in tension; and 3) Releasing the tension with the recap of the melody. It's a tried-and-true statement of musical structure that reaches to new heights within the genre of electric bass.

The word "continuum" is defined as "a link between two things, or a continuous series of things, that blend into each other so gradually and seamlessly that it is impossible to say where one becomes the next" (Webster's Abridged Dictionary, 1999). This definition accurately describes the melody of this piece, as the listener is often unaware of when the first statement ends and the next one begins; they seem to elide one another in a continuous loop.

The melody of "Continuum" has become an anthem for bassists of all skill levels. It represents an archetypical model of composition for bass, complete with fundamental drones, shimmering harmonics, purring fretless melodies, and chordal double-stops. The AAB form begins with a low E and harmonics on C♯, F♯, and B. Jaco is accompanied by keys and light cymbal work, providing unobtrusive harmonic and rhythmic support for his solo.

The first solo begins with a narrow range and hints at the original melody. Rather than jumping out of the gate with a blazing solo, Jaco once again begins to develop and vary the melodic material that's already been presented. The pulse of the solo is based on the quarter note, though a great deal of the phrasing involves quarter-note and eighth-note triplets. Because of this, sixteenth-note runs such as the one in measures 59–60 sound dramatic in contrast. Another one of these runs, found in measures 71–73, features five-note groupings of sixteenth notes that further manipulate the pulse.

Measure 81 marks the beginning of a dramatic build featuring Wes Montgomery-like octave phrasing with quarter-note triplets. This section is a brilliant example of Jaco's unique improvisational style. Over the A6/9 chord in measure 87, he emphasizes E, C♯, and G♯. Over the Cmaj7 in measure 88, he emphasizes B, D, and G, and over the E6/9 in measure 89, he chooses C♯, G♯, F♯, and A♯. As with poetry, where fewer, more meaningful words are chosen, Jaco gets the most out of the handful of notes he chooses to express the harmony. The end of this section is capped with a smooth glissando to an emphatic low E, and before you can catch your breath, Jaco is off and running again with a sixteenth-note ascent to high B. This is answered with an arpeggiated return to low E, effortlessly covering a two and one-half octave range.

Measure 111 begins the recap of the melody that is played almost note-for-note as the beginning, with a few subtle changes in phrasing, ending as peacefully as it began on an E6/9 chord. As with "Donna Lee" and "Portrait of Tracy," "Continuum" has earned its place in the bass canon and continues to inspire and challenge bassists today.

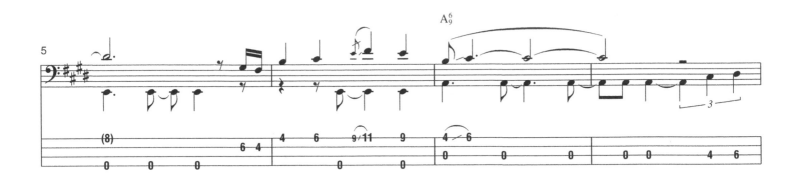

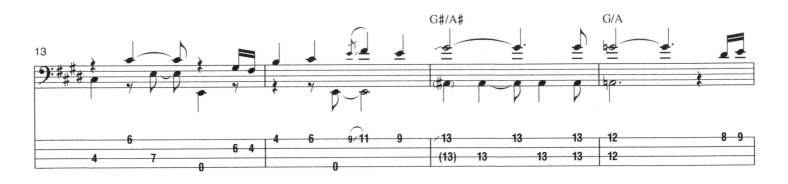

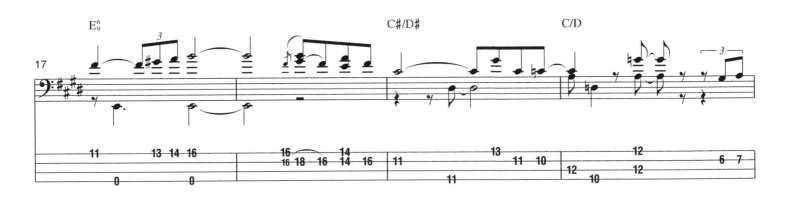

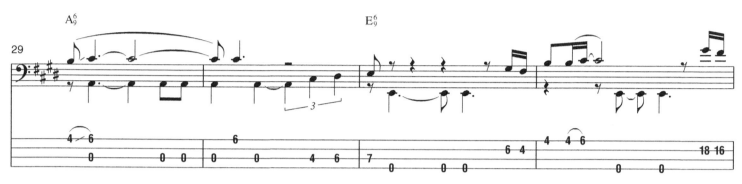

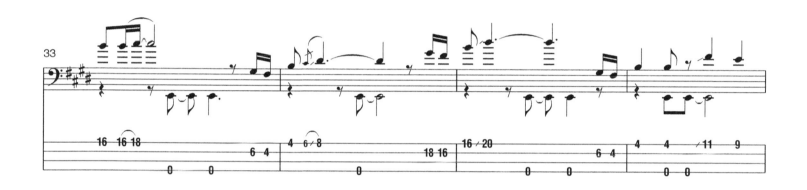

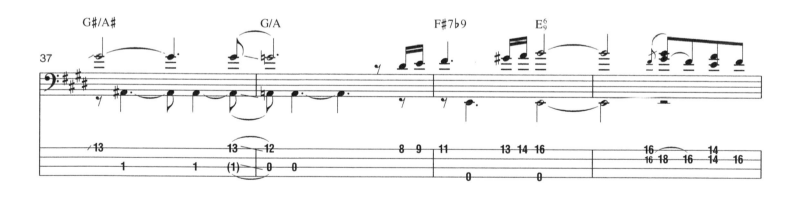

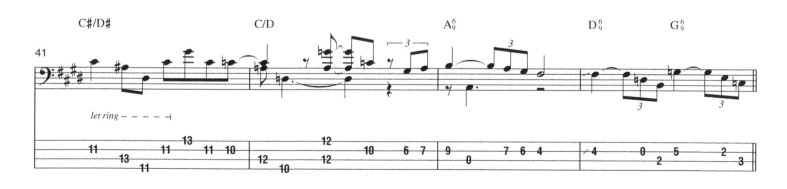

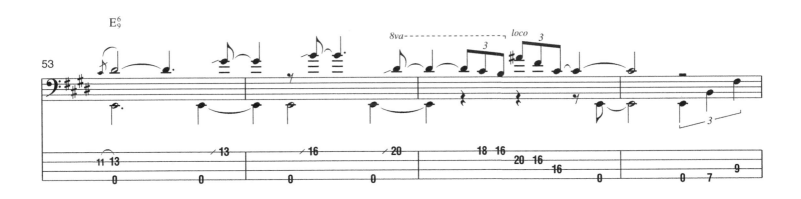

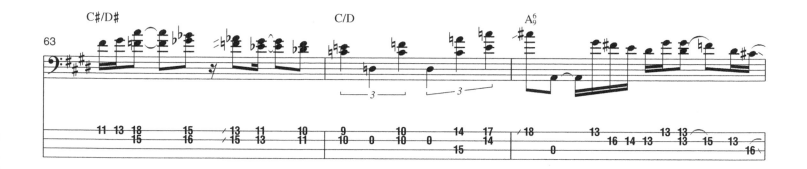

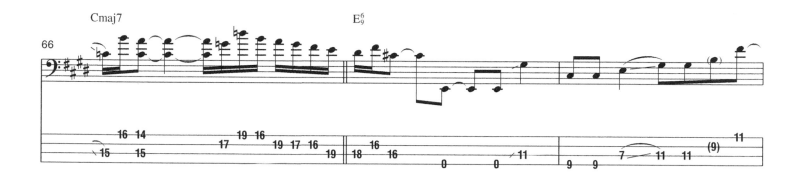

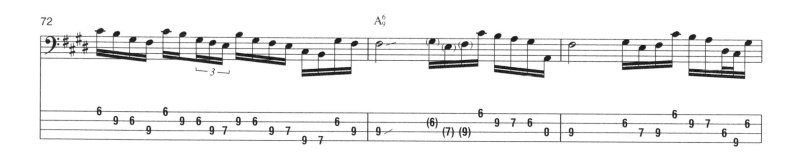

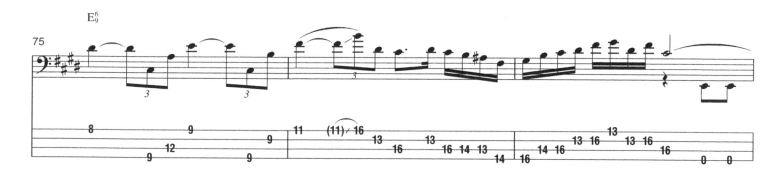

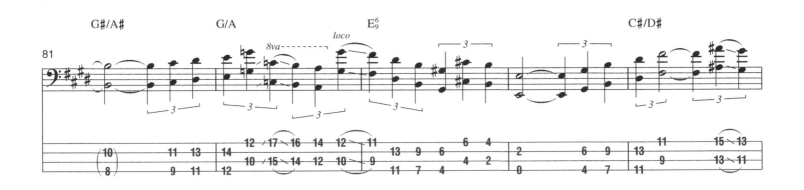

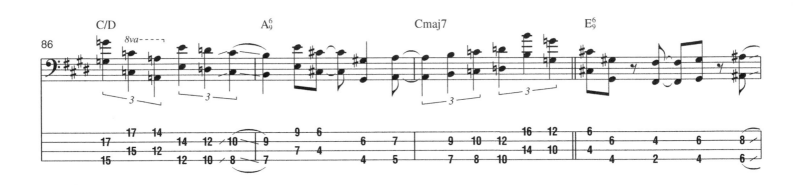

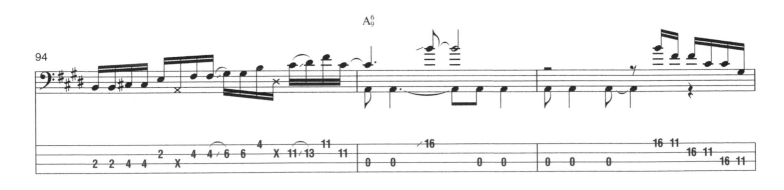

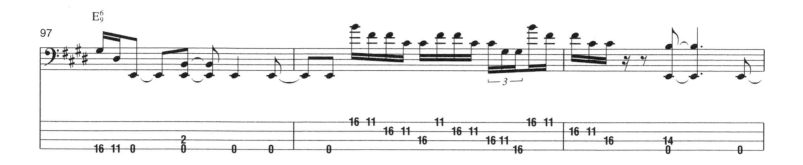

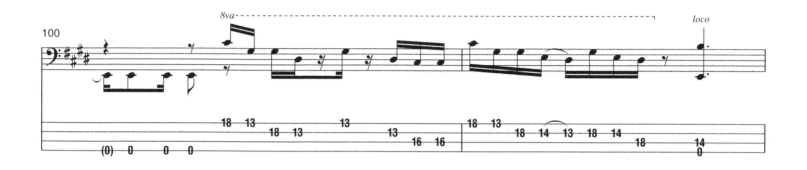

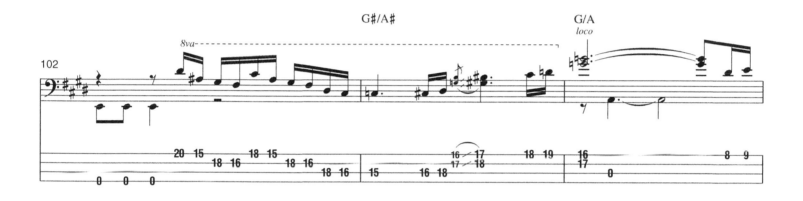

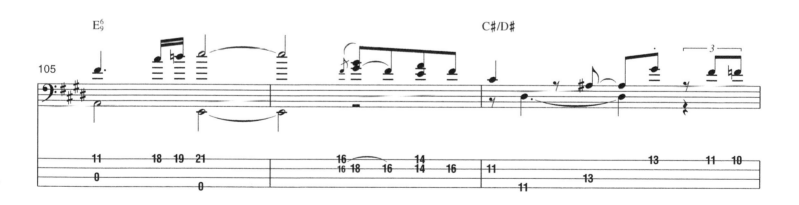

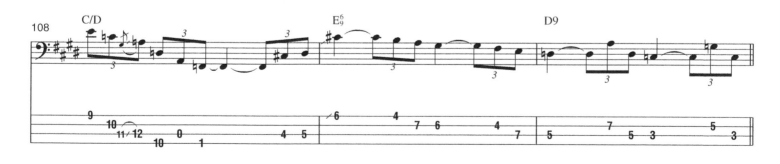

PORTRAIT OF TRACY

By Jaco Pastorius

The natural by-product of a vibrating string is the *overtone series*, a collection of pitches that sound simultaneously with the fundamental. As a string vibrates, it continues to divide into sections—first in half, then thirds, quarters etc. At each of those divisions is a *harmonic node*, where a chime-like tone can be produced when a finger is lightly placed over that spot and the string is plucked. Most commonly, harmonics are used to tune the instrument at the seventh and fifth frets, but Jaco heard more than that, and composed the harmonics masterpiece *Portrait of Tracy*.

The introduction is a cascading motif of harmonics found over the third, fourth, and fifth frets, containing most of the pitch material found in the entire piece. The B section introduces the main theme and features a technique often used by cellists and violinists to achieve *flageolet* notes. In order to create the D♯ harmonic in measure 4, the first finger is placed on the note B, second fret on the A string, and the fourth is placed above the sixth fret. With this technique, the first finger is analogous to the *nut*, and the fourth finger analogous to the fourth fret. The relationship is no different than playing the fourth fret on an open string—like using a moveable capo. This section also features a chord Jaco often used: E♭7♯9 with E♭ as the bass note and G, G♭, and D♭ played as harmonics.

The C section serves as the bridge, producing a descending chromatic bass line from G♯ to E, augmented by three-note harmonic clusters. The D section is a lilting 5/4, featuring two distinct parts: a chromatic bass line (C–B–B♭), with complementary harmonics that fill out the rest of the harmony. The fourth finger plays the bass line, and the harmonics are played with the first, second, and third fingers. The right-hand thumb strikes the E string, while fingers 1 and 2 pluck the harmonics. The harmonics on A and D are doubled on the D and G strings at the fifth and seventh frets, respectively. This requires quite a stretch and some coordination, but the end result is a lush, chorused sound with two independent parts. This section is repeated with increasingly dissonant harmony, generated on the fourth and third frets. It serves as a nice contrast and prepares the return of the main motif. The end of this section contains two chords: one built on B♭, the other on F, with harmonics based on the first and second frets. It's difficult to get these notes to sound; they require a lighter touch for the harmonics and a little heavier touch for the bass notes since they are in first position.

The main motif eventually returns and offers a tonal relief to the dissonant harmony that preceded it. There is a short pause on the E♭7♯9, followed by an Emaj7♯11. This chord is played with the same *flageolet* technique found in the main motif. The first finger of the left hand holds the notes E, B, and F♯ on the ninth fret, while the fourth finger lies gently across the thirteenth fret on the G, D, and A strings. The low E is plucked, and then the three harmonics above create the G♯, D♯, and A♯ to complete the Emaj7♯11 chord. This final chord was doubled with an overdub, creating a shimmering chorus effect.

"Portrait of Tracy" is not only a revelation of the musical use of harmonics, but is a brilliant example of composition for the solo bass guitar and a testament to how much *one* person can get out of *one* instrument. It is much more than just a clever combination of harmonics and fretted notes; it illustrates the entire gamut of timbral possibilities for the electric bass via a tightly-packed, highly-organized structure and an organic melodic framework.

* Chord symbols reflect implied harmony.
** All upstemmed notes are harmonics.
Pitches sound two octaves higher than
written except where indicated at D.

*** D# harmonic is produced by fretting a B on the 2nd fret of the
A string with the index finger, then playing the harmonic on the
6th fret of the A string with the pinky finger while still holding the B.

* Harmonics are located approx. 3/8" past 2nd fret.
** Harmonics are located directly over 2nd fret.

* Applies to harmonics only

* Harmonics are produced by barring the 9th fret
of the G, D and A string with the index finger,
then playing the harmonics on the 13th fret of
the same strings.

(USED TO BE A) CHA CHA

By Jaco Pastorius

The most prominent features of Jaco's solo from his composition "(Used To Be a) Cha-Cha" are precise rhythmic articulation and the use of almost the entire range of the bass. Jaco's sense of time was legendary, and this solo shows us why. The basic pulse of this tune is felt in 2, with the solo subdivided in eighth notes and occasional quarter-note triplets. Each and every note is articulated so cleanly and precisely that there is no question about the intention of every pitch. This is another facet of the Pastorius revolution: highly energized lines with crystal-clear execution spanning the entire bass neck.

Jaco had a knack for emphasizing modal scale degrees, creating tremendous tonal color in his bass lines and especially his solos. Throughout the minor-seventh chords found in this tune, Jaco most often uses the Dorian mode, being sure to emphasize the raised 6th scale degree as he did in measures 1, 4, 13, and so on. Measure 13 features an ascending arpeggio of B half-diminished, then a C♯ and E that resolve to D and A—all over a D minor seventh chord. In this short span, he maximizes the color of the Dorian mode, along with the tension of the leading tone and supertonic, framing the tonic pitch.

In measure 20, Jaco begins hinting at the melody of the tune, highlighting the extensions of the harmony: the 13th, ♭9th, ♯5th, and ♯9th. The phrasing is tight and compact, and there isn't a wasted note. In measure 37, Jaco plays one of his trademark lines, phrasing eighth notes in five-note groups. The pattern ceases in measure 39 where he changes to a four-note grouping, with the beginning of each phrase on the last half of beats 2 and 4, creating a syncopated effect. This descending line—syncopated pentatonic fills grouped in fours—is omnipresent in Jaco's solos.

In measure 57, Jaco plays a four-note pattern of F♯–D–B–A which is transposed almost entirely up a whole step to G♯–E–C–G♯, framing the arrival of the pitch G in measure 58—all over Dm7. Some of the pitches are outside the given harmony, but the organization of the phrasing gives the feeling that the dissonance will resolve at some point, adding tension by creating a goal of the directed motion. At the end of measure 60, Jaco plays a motif consisting of two eighth notes and one quarter note that he sequences through measure 63, displacing it rhythmically. This sort of motivic development provides a unifying quality to the solo, as if each line seems related to previous statements, growing out of one central idea. By measure 89, Jaco begins to restate the melody of the tune as the chordal accompaniment becomes tacit. This prepares a tremendous run from low G♭ to high D♭, consisting of fourths separated by a whole step in three different octaves.

Most of the solos on Jaco's first album share similar qualities: strong rhythmic drive, pristine articulation, colorful modal and chromatic pitch choice, harmonics, pattern-based pentatonic runs, and use of the entire bass range. In addition, all of the improvisation seems to have benefited from a great deal of forethought and planning, whereas later recordings begin to reveal a more "searching" quality, suggesting that more was left up for grabs during the recording process. What they all have in common is an unprecedented virtuosity and sensitivity that transcend the instrument. This was not merely a bassist's solo album; it was the voice of a tremendous musician and composer who happened to play bass. From this point on, the electric bass would never be the same.

Bass solo

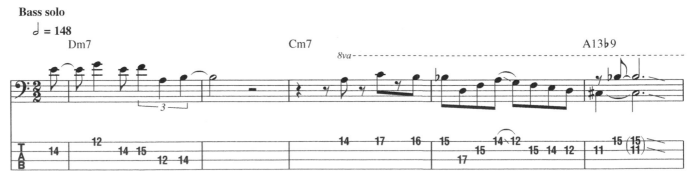

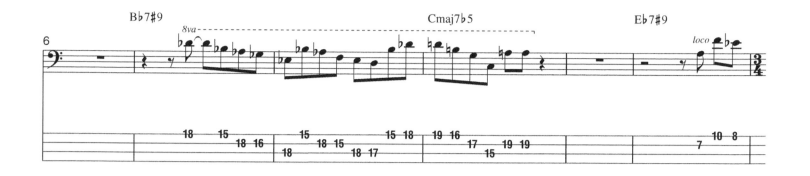

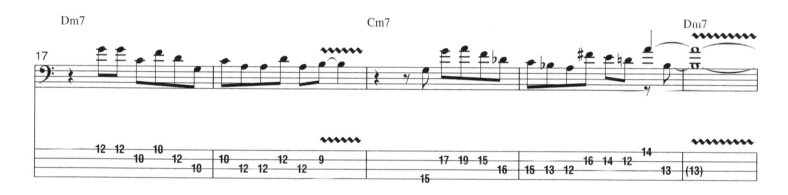

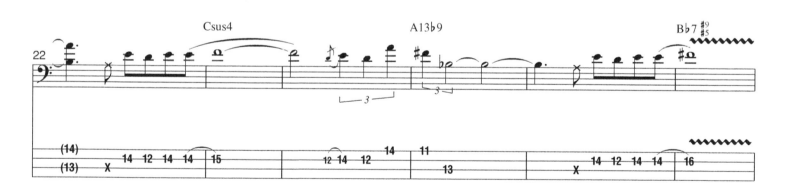

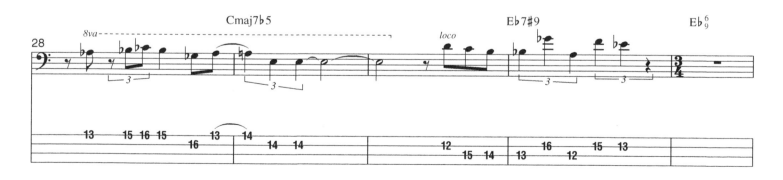

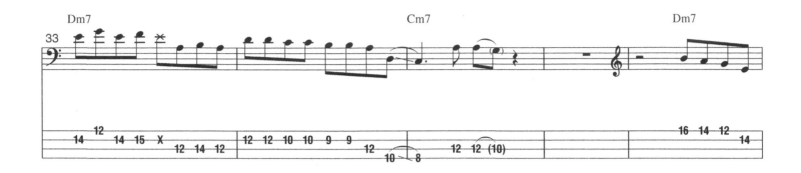

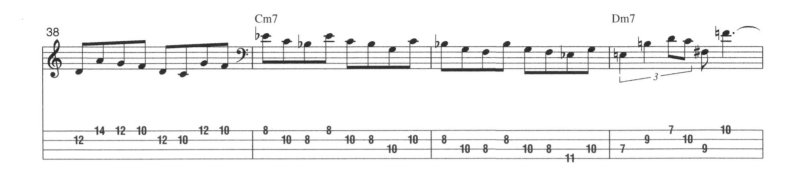

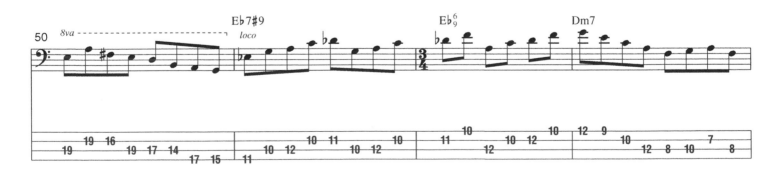

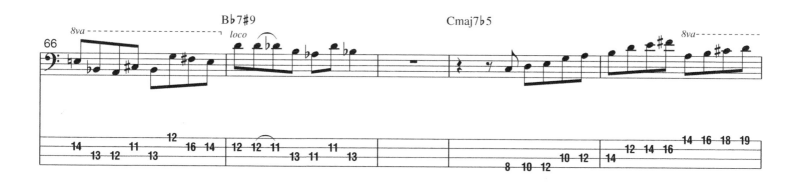

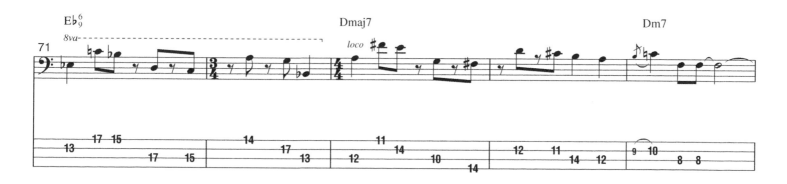

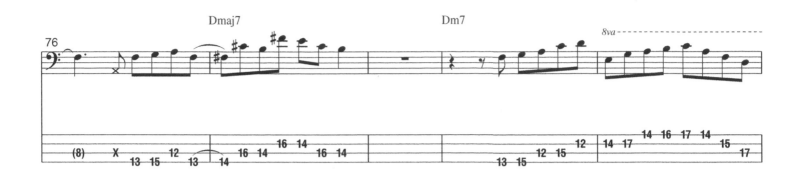

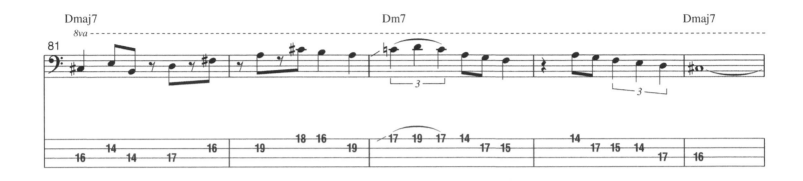

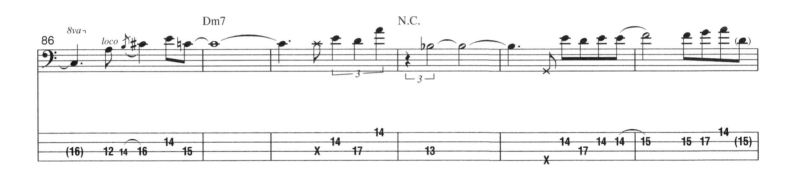

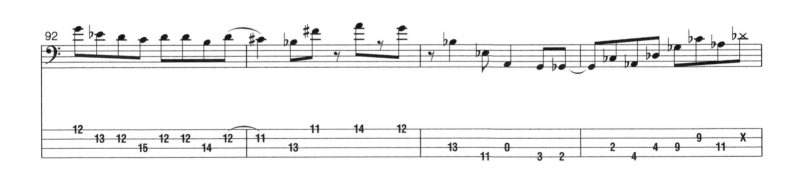

BRIGHT SIZE LIFE

By Pat Metheny

Jaco's solo from the title track of Pat Metheny's debut album, *Bright Size Life*, features a great deal of motivic unity and development, as well as some beautiful legato phrasing. Jaco enters his solo by playing a fragment of the opening theme—a series of 5ths beginning on F♯, continuing on B, E, and D—and introduces a quarter-note triplet figure that he refers to consistently throughout the solo. The first few phrases are restrained and focused on chord tones. By measure 14, Jaco steers away from the triplet quarter notes, favoring eighth notes and a few quarter notes.

In measure 20, a four-note motif is sequenced twice, setting up an eighth-note triplet run from low B to high G. The remainder of this chorus, through measure 33, is less rhythmically strict than the opening two-thirds of the solo. There is a more "searching" quality to it, with looser phrasing and a greater variety of rhythm, including the return of the quarter-note triplet figure in measure 27. The syncopated eighth notes in measures 30 and 31 prepare a restatement of the theme that began the solo.

The second chorus sees even more rhythmic freedom, punctuated with some virtuosic runs. Jaco is still playing very much inside the harmony, subtly passing through chord tones so that the chord progression remains clear. Measures 40 and 41 feature an amazing sixteenth-note run that essentially is an arpeggio of a B♭ major triad combined with a lower-neighbor pattern one semitone beneath each chord tone: B♭–A, D–C♯, F–E, etc. The climax of the run is a high G over a Gmaj7 chord that is quickly arpeggiated downward to facilitate a return to the middle register of the instrument.

In measure 47, Jaco extends the local harmony (D/C) with harmonics on F♯ and B, adding a ♯11th and major 7th. He gracefully ends the phrase with a low B and G, contrasting the high ringing harmonics. Soon afterward, in measure 50, Jaco adds another trademark lick: slurred double stops. He implies an A7 over the G/A chord by playing a high G and C♯, which he planes downward to F and B to accommodate the F/G chord. As the solo begins to wind down, Jaco returns to the quarter-note triplet figure in measures 58–60, played in groups of two and thus creating a hemiola. In this case, he creates the feeling of two within a compound grouping. The solo ends with the same figure that began the tune and his solo.

One quality of great improvisers is their ability to create and release tension via a contour that begins slowly, gradually builds in intensity, and then releases into the next solo or recap of the tune. It's similar to telling a story; elements are presented one-by-one and expanded, building energy and excitement until a climactic point is reached. Jaco's solo in "Bright Size Life" increasingly expands the tune's harmonic and rhythmic boundaries, but they are never completely abandoned. The listener always retains a sense of form and melody, and key harmonic changes are supported by subtle articulation of chord tones.

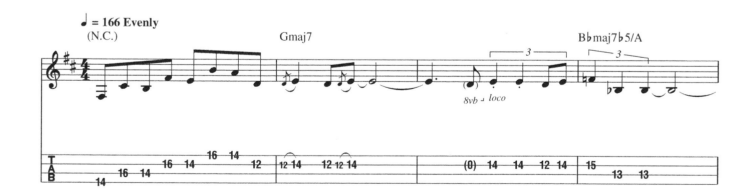

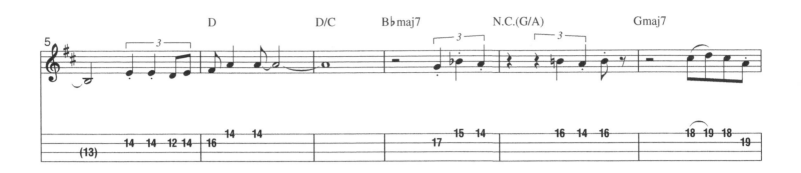

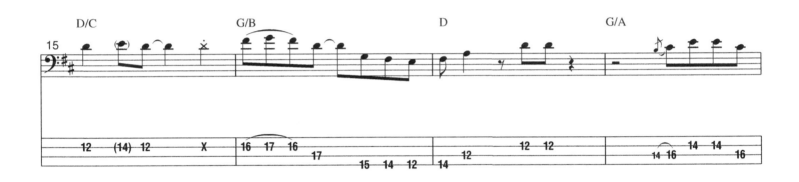

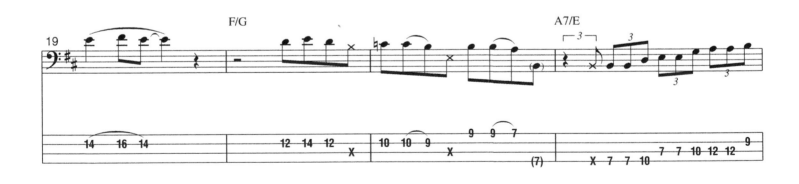

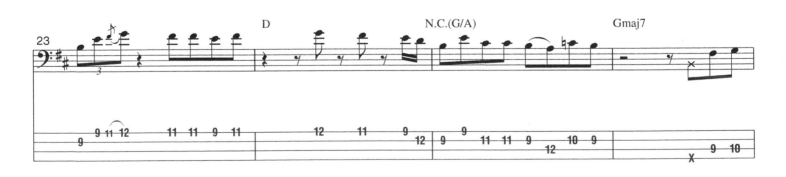

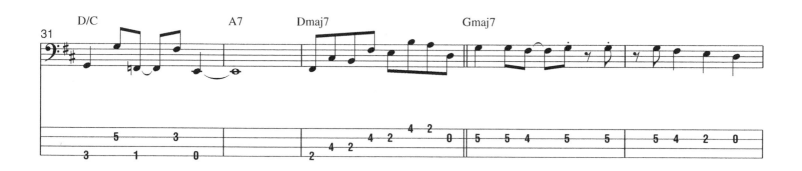

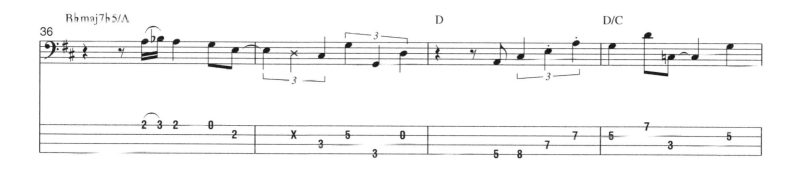

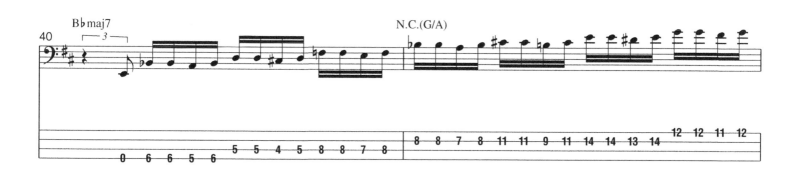

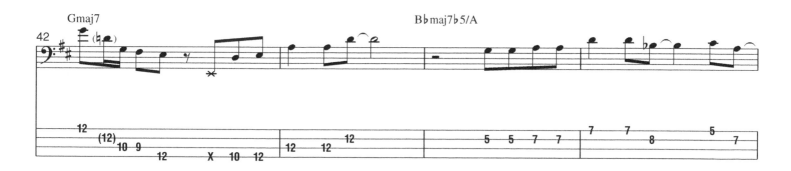

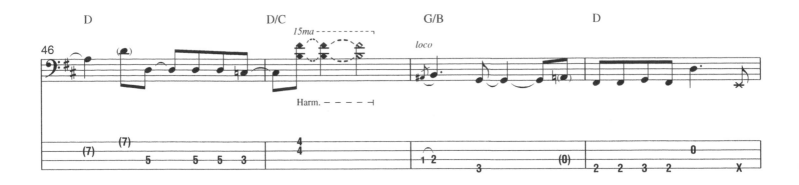

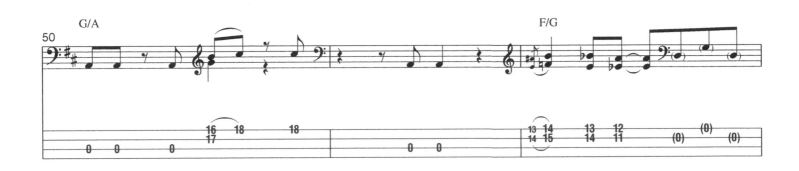

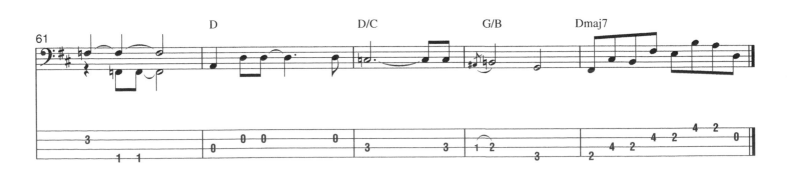

HAVONA

By Jaco Pastorius

Weather Report's *Heavy Weather* was groundbreaking in the newly emerging genre of jazz-rock. The generic term "fusion," often used to describe the music of Weather Report and several other groups from the 1970s, does the music a disservice by lumping it all together, as if it all sounded the same and had the same audience. Jaco contributed two compositions to *Heavy Weather*: the chops-driven "Teen Town" and the Latin-influenced "Havona." Both compositions showcase Jaco's bass playing, but it is the latter that documents his maturity as a composer.

Each phrase of Jaco's solo is clear-cut and complete; each was constructed in the studio and reportedly punched in one-at-a-time. Present is Jaco's incredible command of the instrument, as well as his melodic and motivic fluency. Part of his "sound" includes an approach to note choice that emphasizes either modal degrees or upper extensions of the harmony, while de-emphasizing the local tonic pitch. Jaco's phrasing is proprietary and innovative; it was articulated from a bassist's point of view, but it serves as a model for any instrumentalist.

The first two statements of Jaco's solo are related motivically, the second being a variation of the first. Measures 5 and 6 feature an unexpected quote from the opening motif in Igor Stravinsky's *The Rite of Spring*, transposed down one half step from the original. Jaco was always eager to wear his influences on his sleeve and to practice the motto attributed to Stravinsky: "A good musician borrows, a great musician *steals*." By measure 12, Jaco summons an old stand-by: descending scalar patterns grouped in fours and fives. B minor pentatonic runs fill out the end of the first chorus, and Jaco decides to remain tacit for the large arpeggio that he had previously played in unison with the piano.

The beginning of the second chorus contains one of the most interesting lines (measures 23 and 24) of the entire solo. The harmony is Cmaj7, and Jaco touches upon the pitch C primarily in metrically weak positions. He emphasizes colorful scale degrees such as the raised 4th, the 6th, the major 7th, and the 9th. It has the effect of sounding "in," but without the constraints that tertian chords imply. By measure 29, the solo has built a considerable amount of momentum, phrased almost entirely in sixteenth notes. The contour of Jaco's line is very wide—from low G to high A in measure 29, to low D♯ in measure 30, back up to high G in measure 31, then down to low G♯ at the start of measure 33. It is here that he may be quoting the first phrase from Pat Metheny's *Bright Size Life* (transposed up one whole step).

Jaco gracefully exits the solo with two bars of continuous triplets, creating a slowing effect on the forward motion. This culminates in the dotted-eighth/sixteenth figure layered with 5ths and octaves in measures 37 and 39, respectively. Jaco plays a unison run with the piano in measure 42, heralding the transition back to the top of the form. A beautifully crafted tune combined with a high-powered bass line and a virtuosic solo make "Havona" a potent example of Jaco's imposing skill and full-compass musicianship.

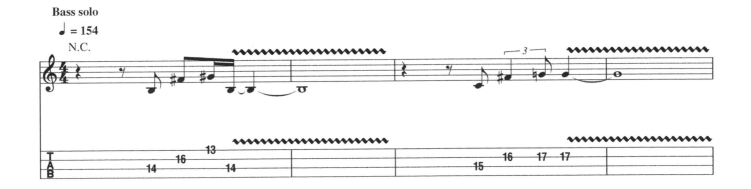

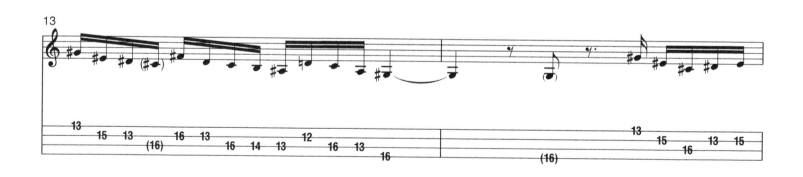

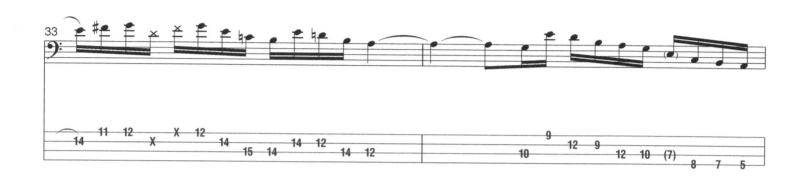

PUNK JAZZ

By Jaco Pastorius

The solos in this collection come in several shapes and sizes, from sublime melodicism to distorted harmonics. Most of the solos have a harmonic foundation as well as a sense of boundary, even if they are unaccompanied; no matter how far "out" Jaco goes, there is still some semblance of "in." The solos from "Punk Jazz" and "Port of Entry," however, are two archetypical examples of when Jaco was, simply put, *ripping.*

"Punk Jazz" is Jaco's own composition, found on the Weather Report album *Mr. Gone.* The title comes from the term Jaco used to describe his own music. (He claimed he was using the term 'punk' long before it became associated with the movement that yielded bands such as The Sex Pistols and The Clash.) An interesting feature of this solo is that it contains few of the patterns and licks Jaco often relied upon; instead, he employs bebop-like lines combined with a rock-like feel—truly "punk jazz."

There is no specific harmonic progression during the opening bass cadenza, but there are extended passages where key areas can be discerned. There are two large sections that comprise this tune: groups of 33 and 34 measures, respectively, divided by a loud and highly reverberated drum accent. The most striking features of Jaco's playing are the speed and accuracy. The notes are clear and distinct, covering the range of low E through high D. At times, lengthy runs are facilitated by the use of the open G string, providing a means to shift position. The downside of this is that the timbre of the open string seems to jump out—a twangy anomaly amidst warmly fingered notes. Be that as it may, it does nothing to detract from this ear-dazzling solo. Measures 63–64 contain what might be a transposed quote from John Coltrane's "Giant Steps."

Each phrase, separated on either side by rests, has its own syntax and vocabulary. For example, measures 34 through 40 are primarily tetrachords connected by intermittent stepwise motion. It is a lengthy phrase and one of the most sequential—one motivic idea, or *subject*, commented upon many times with slight variation. Think of it as a conversation in which the speaker makes a concept or idea clearer by use of analogy—it's basically the same *thing*, just presented in a variety of ways. We understand the core or the essence of the idea as it is preserved from statement to statement via the contour, interval choice, and rhythm. Measures 45–48 contain a shorter phrase featuring larger intervals that ascend and alternately descend—a kind of crest and trough that provides a sense of balance. These kinds of organizational features subconsciously contribute to our perception of the phrase's meaning; rather than being perceived simply as a collection of random pitches, Jaco's solo conveys a palpable degree of intent and purpose.

A transcription such as this offers a glimpse into the creative mind of an improviser at the moment of expression. By playing this piece, we put ourselves in Jaco's place and experience a musical vocabulary vastly different than our own. Perhaps the most interesting aspect of studying this solo is deciphering Jaco's choice of notes. If it was truly improvised, why were these notes chosen over others? What was Jaco trying to communicate? Proper answers to these questions far exceed the scope of this book, but serve as a point of departure for further study and dissemination.

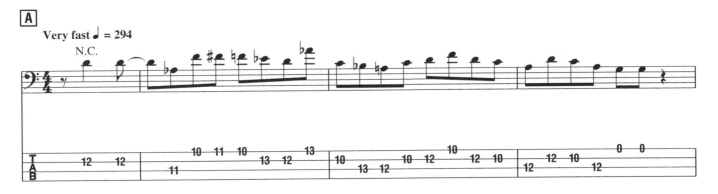

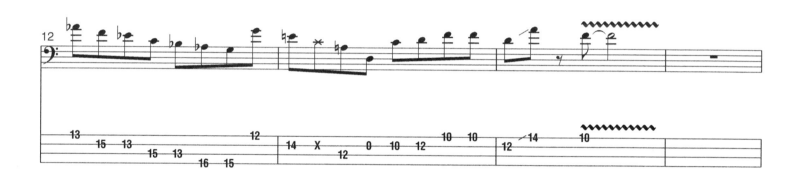

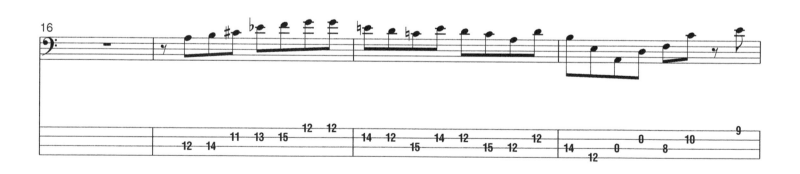

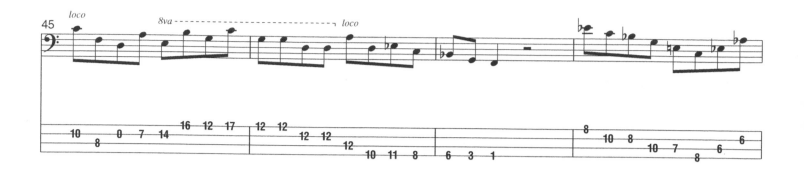

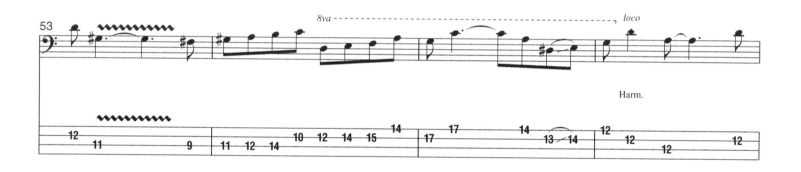

SLANG

By Jaco Pastorius

A feature of every Weather Report concert was a solo performance by each of the musicians. "Slang" is a live recording of what many thousands of fans heard Jaco play during his years of touring. Most, if not all of you, are familiar with the classic joke: "beware of when the drums stop—*bass solo!*" And that joke isn't unfounded, so the idea of a solo electric bass performance was less than appealing to most. What could possibly be played on solo electric bass that could be considered actual music *and* keep the audience's attention for more than five minutes? It turns out that there is plenty to say and quite a show to see. Enter Jaco Pastorius—part Sid Vicious, part Jimi Hendrix, part Charlie Parker, and part Wilson Pickett.

The order of events became standardized in a Pastorius bass solo: some high-register melodic work, often including a variety of musical quotes, followed by a repeating bass loop over which Jaco often quotes Jimi Hendrix, then a feedback-driven explosion of distorted harmonics, capped off with some more melodic work, and for good measure, a hearty back-flip off of his amplifier onto his bass. "Slang" would silence all doubters and add another chapter to the Pastorius revolution.

Jaco begins "Slang" with a melody starting on low F and intersperses harmonics, which sound out some favorite Pastorius chords: E7#9, Bm7, and Bb13. He then takes off with some blazing, albeit rough, chromatic lines that are part blues and part bebop. This section ends with a diminished seventh arpeggio and some phrasing that is reminiscent of his work on "Donna Lee."

The next section of the solo is considered to be an innovation on Jaco's part, though anecdotal evidence supports that Jaco got the idea from Alphonso Johnson. Jaco slaps his bass strings with an open palm over the pickup while engaging a delay pedal that has the ability to repeat infinitely . This provides the tempo for Jaco's layered, three-part motif that creates the harmonic and rhythmic foundation over which he'll solo. The motif consists essentially of the extensions of an E9 chord (B–D–F#) and includes their upper neighbors (C#–E–G#) as well. Once he establishes all of the layering, he hits the "repeat" function and becomes a one-man-band. He equalizes the tone of the loop, preparing the next section of his solo.

Jaco plays a handful of licks in the upper register, mixing legato and staccato statements with the low E string. Most of the lines are mainly pentatonic and/or bluesy in a funk setting. At this point, he engages the distortion pedal and flies into a rendition of the Jimi Hendrix classic "Third Stone from the Sun." The audience usually responds with shock and amazement, which ushers them into a new level of engagement with the solo. The Hendrix section of the solo winds down with a large, deliberate slide down the bass neck, and Jaco returns to a clean tone, referring back to the melodic material he presented earlier.

The final section is announced by disengaging the bass loop and playing a Cmaj9 chord with harmonics and a low C. Jaco then quotes the first phrase from his composition "Portrait of Tracy" and slides deftly into a quote from "The Sound of Music." After his trademark Eb7#9 chord, a distorted low A sounds for a few seconds, followed by a crash on a distorted low E. This is the point where Jaco has undoubtedly jumped off his amplifier, generating a roar of applause from the audience.

If we stand back and inventory the contents of "Slang," we get funk, bebop, Jimi Hendrix, and a dash of Julie Andrews, all combined with the showmanship that's part James Brown and part Barnum's Circus. The playing itself is enough to convince any listener of Jaco's enormous skill and talent, but combine that with the stage presence and the aura that surrounded him, and it's easy to understand why Jaco became larger than life. A point that is often overlooked with Jaco is that it wasn't only his playing ability that made him a virtuoso; it was also the virtuosity of his creativity and an innate ability and desire to entertain. In other words, "Slang" worked because Jaco *made* it work.

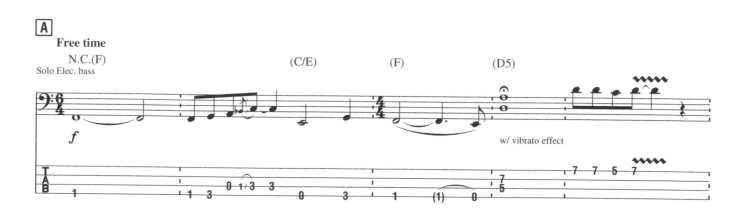

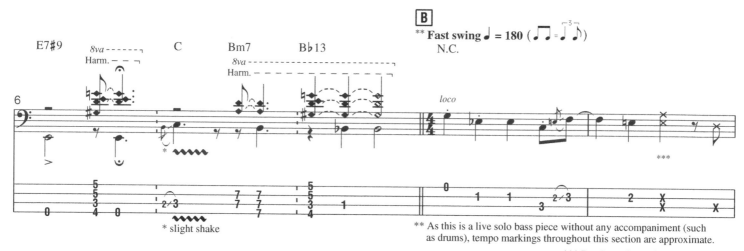

** As this is a live solo bass piece without any accompaniment (such as drums), tempo markings throughout this section are approximate.

*** Deaden strings with plucking hand.

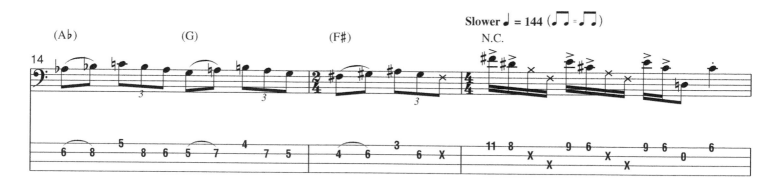

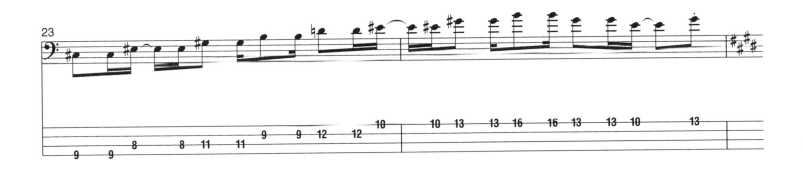

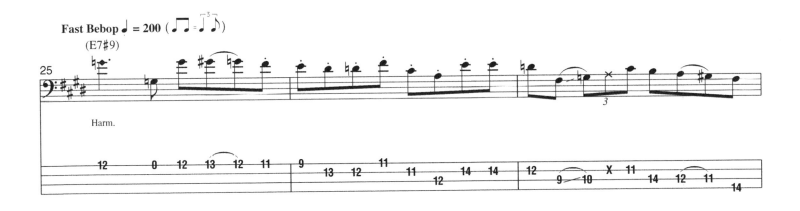

Moderate Funk feel ♩ = 108

N.C.

* P.M. ------------┐

* Pluck string w/ thumb while muting with the heel of the plucking hand.

** This section is performed with an infinite delay effect timed to half notes. Upstemmed cue-sized notes and tab numbers in parentheses indicate echo repeats. (The effect on the recording can be emulated by running the echo signal through a second slightly overdriven amplifier with the bass control turned down and the midrange control turned up.)

E9

Bass Loop 1

Play 8 times

End Bass Loop 1

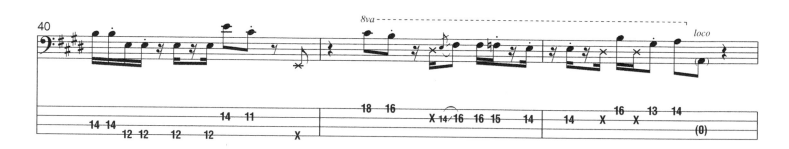

*** Slap deadened strings percussively with plucking hand.

w/ Bass Loop 1 (17 times)

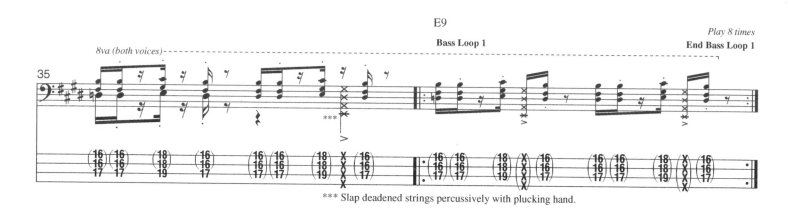

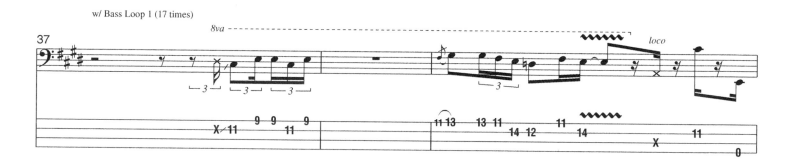

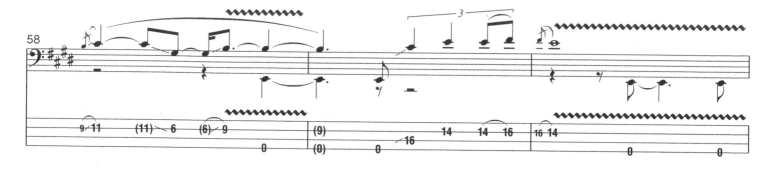

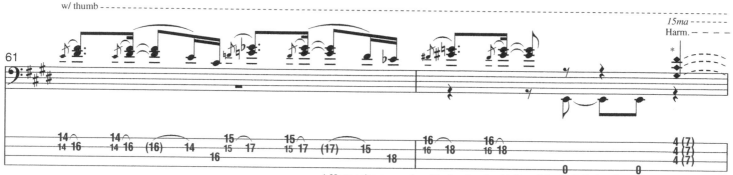

* Harmonics are produced by barring the 4th fret of the G, D & A strings with the index finger,
then playing the harmonics on the 7th fret of the same strings with the pinky finger (while
still holding the notes on the 4th fret).

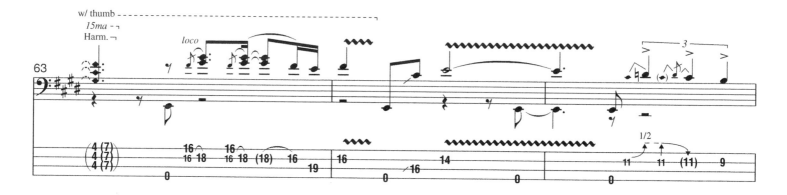

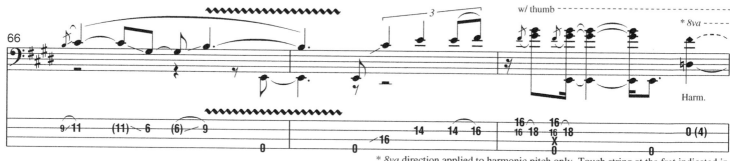

* 8va direction applied to harmonic pitch only. Touch string at the fret indicated in
parentheses very lightly so as to allow both the harmonic and the string to ring.

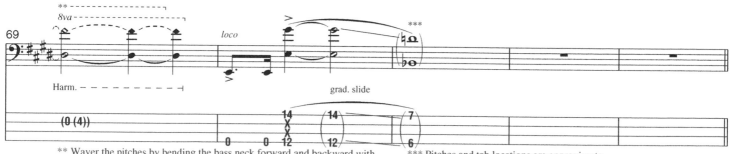

** Waver the pitches by bending the bass neck forward and backward with
the fretting hand while anchoring the bass body with the plucking hand.

*** Pitches and tab locations are approximate.

* All upstemmed notes are harmonics. Pitches sound one octave higher than written,

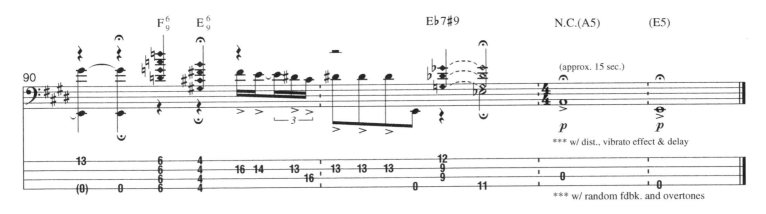

* D♯ harmonic is produced by fretting a B on the 2nd fret of the A string with the index finger, then playing the harmonic on the 6th fret of the A string with the pinky finger (while still holding the B).

** Touch string at the fret indicated in parentheses very lightly so as to allow both the harmonic and the open string to ring.

*** w/ dist., vibrato effect & delay

*** w/ random fdbk. and overtones

PORT OF ENTRY

By Wayne Shorter

The song "Port of Entry," composed by Wayne Shorter, is found on Weather Report's *Night Passage*. The song structure can be divided into three main sections: a slow opening section containing the main melody, a double-time bass and percussion solo, then a recap of the melody over the double-time feel; a small tag caps the piece. Jaco, using false harmonics, doubles the first presentation of the melody and follows it with a deep but sparse groove in C major, which leads to the bass solo. Harmonically, Jaco's solo strays from C major but remains largely pentatonic. The rhythmic accuracy and clarity of the pitches, combined with a slightly distorted tone, adds a sense of urgency to the performance and is one of the finest examples of Jaco's monstrous technical ability.

The first two statements are almost exact transpositions of each other: the second statement a perfect fourth lower than the first. After a short lick in A minor (measure 6), Jaco follows with the first of many pentatonic runs. The phrasing includes groups of four notes sequenced on the pitches G–C–A–G. In measure 18, Jaco introduces a motif of arpeggiated seventh chords, which descend in whole-step increments. The first three statements are metrically separated by an eighth-note rest, after which Jaco compresses the motif to occur every quarter note. The first set of descending seventh chords includes Dm7, Gm7, and Bm7. The second set, in measure 20, consists of Dm7, C7, Cm7, and Bm7. This sequence is interesting because instead of simply planing the shape of the seventh chord downward, Jaco shifted from C7 to Cm7, then on to Bm7. The chords aren't related by key, and the subtle adjustment enhances an otherwise predictable sequence.

Measure 26 features another lengthy pentatonic run, though this time Jaco plays groupings of five notes that creates a polyrhythm between the bass and drums. By accenting every fifth note, the tempo appears to be slower, which gives the illusion that something is slowing down despite the fact the sixteenth notes are played at the same tempo. Supporting this effect is the fact that pentatonic scales consist of five notes, so each statement has a sense of completeness to it, reinforcing the arrival of each new "beat." Only a performer with the most precise sense of meter can pull this off, otherwise it sounds like a conflict in the rhythm section.

A new melodic grouping, consisting of a descending 3rds followed by two consecutive 2nds, sequenced by an ascending second, occurs in measure 32. The building tension of the continuous ascent is finally released in measures 34 and 35, ending with another one of Jaco's trademark licks: parallel 3rds descending by step. The goal of this motion is the pitch A, which Jaco holds for one and a half measures, preparing the arrival of the third large section of the tune. At the end of Jaco's solo, the listener is expecting change, and Jaco's climax is a means of backing out from all of the energy, so that the transition feels smooth and natural.

If nothing else, Jaco's performance on "Port of Entry" raises the bar for technical achievement on the bass guitar, but it's much more than that. Providing a sense of unity and cohesion in a solo is a challenge for any improviser, especially when there is no supporting harmony. Part and parcel to a sense of cohesion is the ability to enter and exit from a solo so that it appears to be part of some larger structure, not just a chance to "wiggle your fingers." Jaco achieves all of these things, while simultaneously infusing his very unique brand of musicianship and creativity.

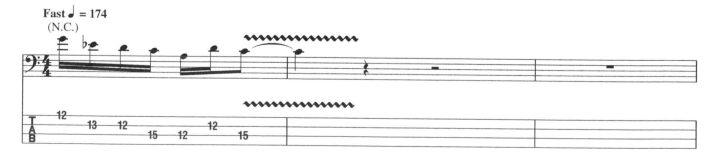

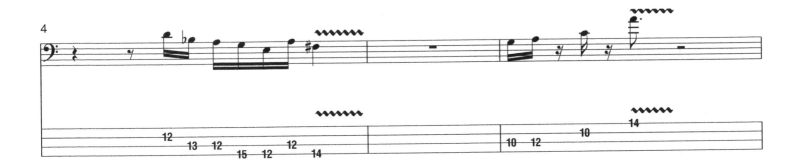

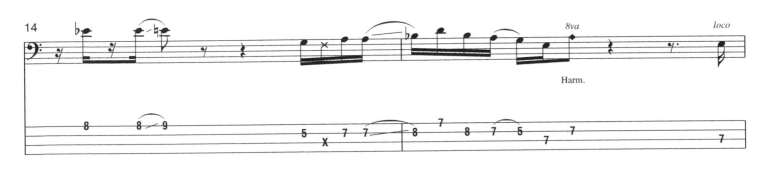

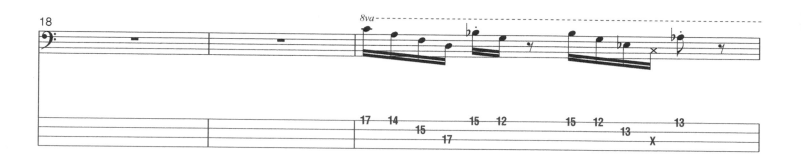

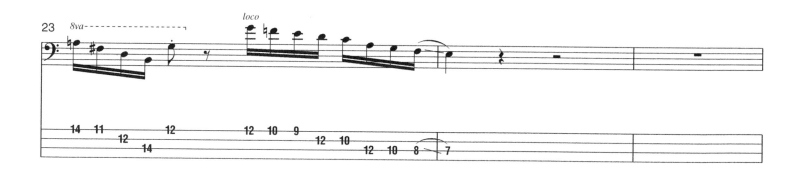

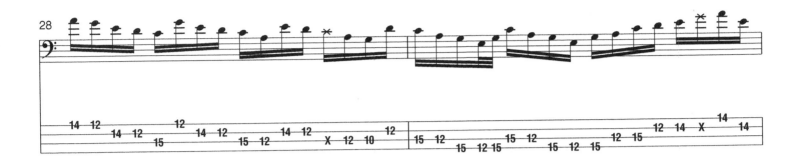

CHROMATIC FANTASY

Arranged by Jaco Pastorius

On the afternoon of July 28, 1750, Johann Sebastian Bach lay dying; having dictated his final piece to his son-in-law Altnikol, he began to hear the first whispers of eternity. With his passing, we would mark the end of the Baroque era and inherit a musical legacy that attained galactic dimensions. Arguably the greatest architect of music, Bach crafted a body of work of such unimaginable intellectual depth and universal beauty that it defies the rigors of time and remains a source of perpetual inspiration. Jaco, like thousands if not millions of others, found inspiration in Bach's music and documented it with his recording of the "Chromatic Fantasy."

The two qualities of Bach's music that contribute most to its universality and longevity are a focus on process and its own internal logic. As a result, his music can be rendered on almost any musical instrument without suffering any aesthetic loss; the focus is on the notes and structure, not the instrument. The Paganini Caprices lose something when not played on violin, just as the Chopin Études suffer when not played on piano; their aesthetic delivery depends heavily upon the instruments for which they're written. So it was only natural for Jaco to record a composition by Bach on electric bass—but we usually find bassists choosing from the Six Suites for Cello, certainly not the imposing "Chromatic Fantasy."

The late Canadian pianist Glenn Gould, considered the foremost interpreter of Bach's works for keyboard, commented that the "Fantasy" is "...our best glimpse at Bach the improviser versus Bach the organizer." A fantasy, or *phantasia*, is an instrumental work whose form and inspiration come solely from the one who composed it. They are usually very free and highly improvisational, but do retain a more or less recognizable sectional form. The entirety of the "Fantasy" is actually much larger than what we find on Jaco's second solo recording, *Word of Mouth*. He only performs the first large section of the piece, as the rest is almost completely unplayable on the bass guitar.

Jaco's touch is very light throughout in order to accommodate the dramatic shifting required of the piece. In addition, he changed the register of a few notes in order to keep it within reachable space on the bass guitar. It's an enormously challenging piece to tackle, but a tremendous gift awaits those who make their way through it. This rendition adds to the growing list of remarkable feats Jaco performed on the instrument, and it is a heartfelt tribute to who was perhaps the greatest musician of all time.

AMERIKA

By Jaco Pastorius

Jaco's third solo album was a live recording of his Word of Mouth Band and was released as a double LP in Japan called *Twins I & II*, referring to the birth of his twin boys. In the United States, the album was packaged as a single LP under the name *Invitation*. Both versions contain Jaco's solo bass arrangement of "America the Beautiful." As "Portrait of Tracy" and "Continuum" showcase Jaco's gifts as a composer for solo bass, "Amerika" is an example of his boundless imagination as an arranger. The result is a remarkable, *cantabile* rendition of an otherwise unremarkable folk tune.

Perhaps the most striking feature of this performance is the sensitivity of Jaco's touch. The gentle glissandi, slurs, and legato runs defy the innate awkwardness of the electric bass. The first phrase is decorated by harmonics on G♯, D, and F♯ over the chord E7. The addition of harmonics is an integral part of the texture, buffeted against the low E and A strings, with the main melody performed predominantly in the middle range. The voice-leading at the end of the first phrase includes a chromatic ascent in the bass, implying the harmonic progression A–F♯7/A♯–E/B–C+, via a subtle contrapuntal second voice.

The end of the second phrase, measure 15, contains a secondary dominant 9th chord that leads to the arrival of E major. Here, Jaco uses his right hand to hammer on the bass note B on the E string, as his left hand holds the three-note chord D♯–A–C♯. The run in measure 17 is a highly decorated approach to the pitch C♯ in measure 18, executed with flawless technique. Jaco alters the articulation of the melody in measures 21–24 by way of false harmonics—placing the thumb of the right hand halfway between the fretted note and the bridge, then plucking behind it with the right-hand index finger. In measure 25, the bass note A is followed by G♯, which could be considered the 3rd of E7 (the V chord in A), and is then followed by an E♭7♯9 chord that resolves to the subdominant, D major. So beneath the active melody, there is a descending bass line A–E (implied)–E♭–D. A reduction of the voice- leading would look like this:

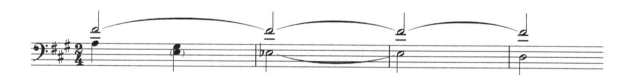

The final phrase of the melody is accompanied by yet another chromatic bass line, ascending in half steps, implying a circle of fifths progression: D–B7/D♯–E–C♯7/E♯, resolving to F♯m. Jaco follows this gentle, poignant statement with the subdominant, D major, and ends the piece with a rapid one-octave scale in A. This moving rendition of "America the Beautiful" would become one of Jaco's hallmarks and is yet another example of the range of expression solo electric bass has to offer.

Tempo Rubato

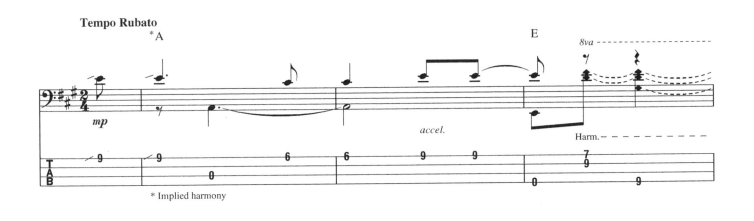

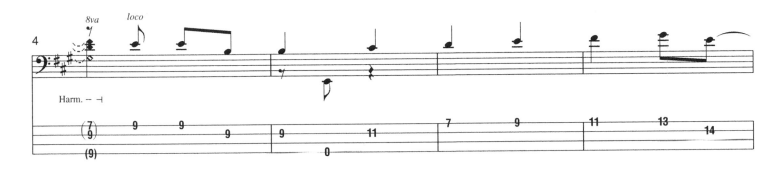

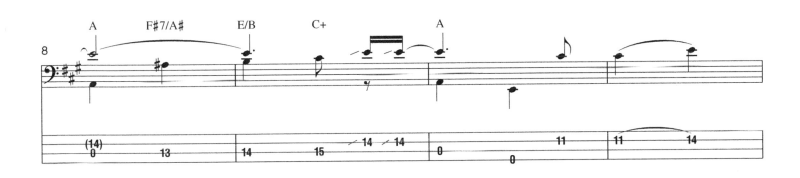

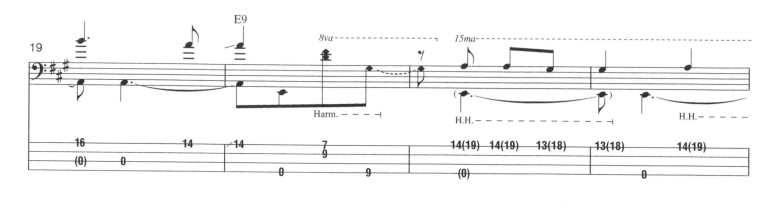

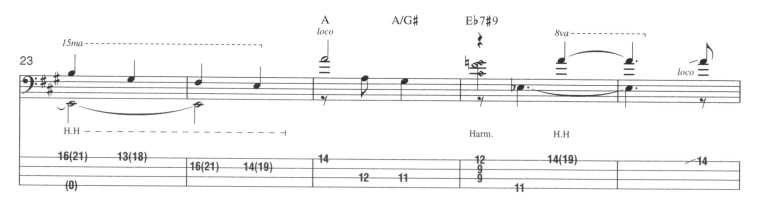

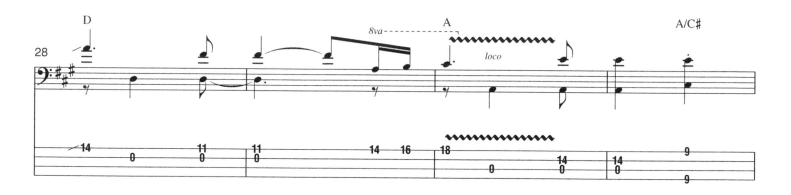

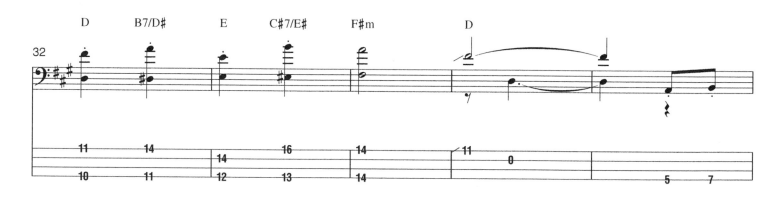

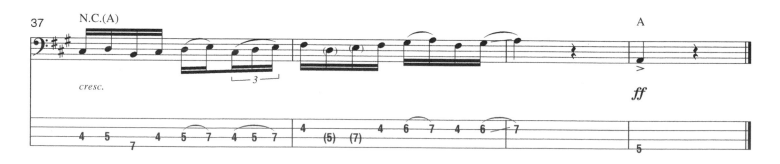

DAYS OF WINE AND ROSES

Lyric by Johnny Mercer
Music by Henry Mancini

In the summer of 1986, Jaco traveled to the West Coast to play some club dates with drummer Brian Melvin, with whom he made contact a few years prior. Together they made several recordings, including what was to be Jaco's last—*Standards Zone*. Pianist Jon Davis joined Pastorius and Melvin for a CD comprised of well-known jazz standards, such as Tadd Dameron's "If You Could See Me Now," and Henry Mancini's "Days of Wine and Roses." This is the first time Jaco was featured in a trio setting, and his playing is hardly reminiscent of the youthful abandon found in his first trio recording, *Bright Size Life*. Instead, the performances are more subdued and restrained, perhaps the result of a lifetime's worth of experiences during the intervening ten years.

Jaco solos through two choruses of the form, predominantly supporting the harmony by including chord tones. The first chorus consists mainly of eighth-note phrasing, while the second chorus is a mixture of eighths, triplets, and sixteenth-note runs. In addition, the second chorus is more fragmentary, with shortened phrases and little motivic development.

In the first chorus, measure 13 features a dotted-quarter/eighth-note figure descending by half step, alternately covering the 7th and 3rd of Em7b5, A7b9, Dm7, G7. The phrase continues with a Bb for the Gm7 chord, but a short pause before it breaks up the predictability of the sequence. Jaco adds a b9 over the C7 chord, plays through the turnaround, and extends the Eb7 chord in measure 18 by adding the 9th (F) and 11th (Ab). From measure 7 through measure 24, there is very little breathing room, creating a continuous flow of melodic ideas. In measure 24, Jaco utilizes the often-used triplets phrased in groups of five. Despite his frequent use of this device, the effect is no less dramatic. As the turnaround approaches, Jaco wears his influences on his sleeve and tags the ending with a figure from the Jimi Hendrix song "The Wind Cries Mary"—though he decorates it with a root–5th–9th pattern.

The second chorus begins with an F major pentatonic fill, followed by three measures that contain only a few staccato eighth notes. Measure 38 features a rather indeterminate sixteenth-note run that partly destabilizes the pulse, but it is soon re-established in measures 40–43. In measure 45, Jaco plays a descending arpeggio mixing eighth notes and eighth-note triplets that he sequences down one half step in the following measure. Measures 47–51 seem the least organized, as Jaco stabs in and out of the harmony until measure 52. At measure 58, he begins winding down the solo by using larger note values, primarily playing the root notes of the harmony. In measure 63, he once again plays the Hendrix tag, preparing the return of the melody.

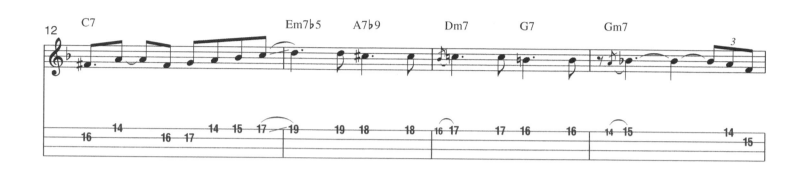

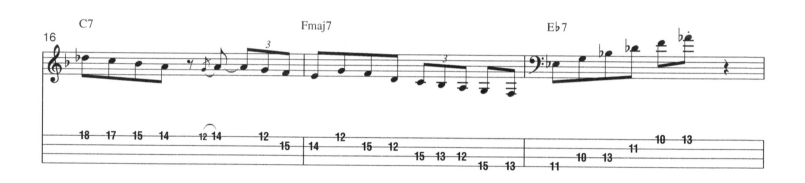

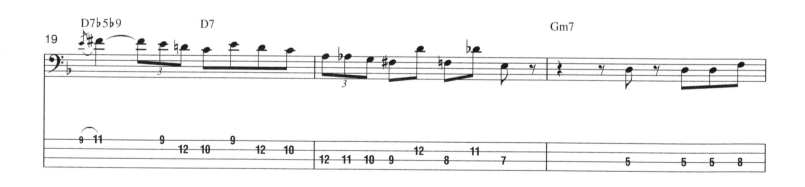

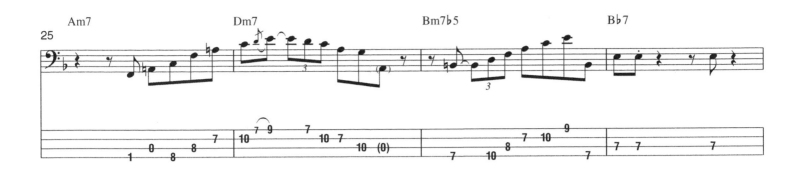

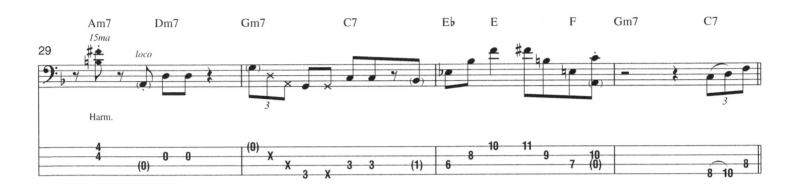

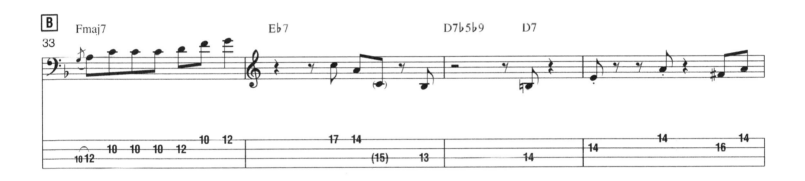

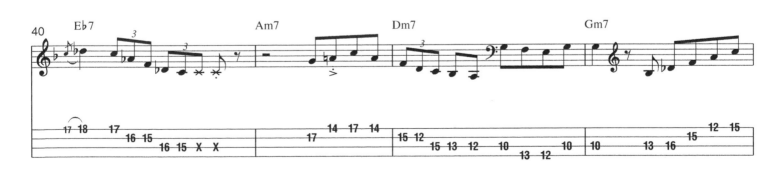

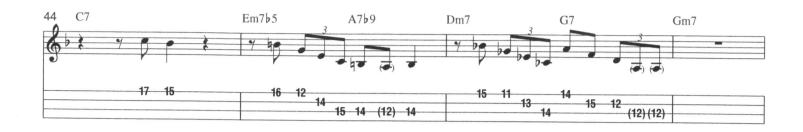

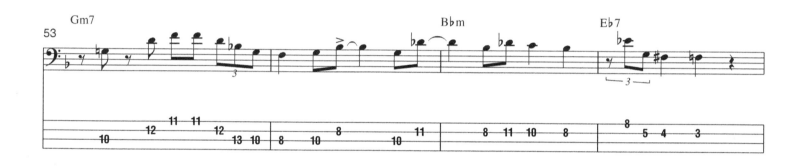

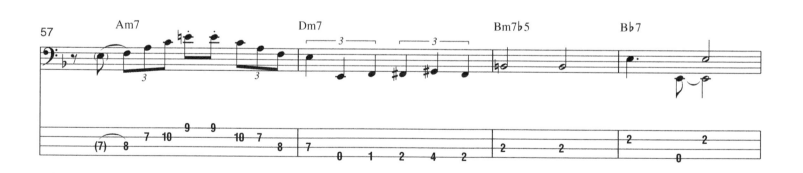

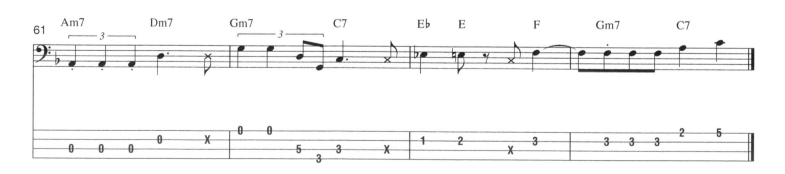

CONCLUSION

A consistent quality of the solos late in Jaco's career is that they start out rather strong, begin to wander a bit, and then consist mainly of patterns and licks that Jaco used all the time. Compare the style and technique of the "Days of Wine and Roses" solo with that of "(Used To Be a) Cha Cha" or "Donna Lee." Even during his years with Weather Report, his solo bass work seemed to plateau conceptually, though it never weakened physically. This is something Jaco himself commented on, stating in a 1983 interview "I'm still using the same [stuff] that I played eight years ago." Throughout his entire career, his impeccable sense of time and rapid-fire chops remained, but as the years went by, he relied more and more on ideas from the past. This is not a criticism *per se*—rather, it's a commentary on an interesting property of prodigy and innovation; after the initial flash of creation, innovators have the tendency to orbit around their primary contribution. In Jaco's case, his initial offering revolutionized *every* aspect of the instrument, which took the audience several years to apprehend. Once the world caught up with him, and bassists all over were copping his style, he was assimilated into a global musical lexicon and no longer received the credit for his innovations. This, combined with manic depression and addiction, affected Jaco's ability to further develop his craft. Despite the manifold number of stories that perpetuate the Pastorius mythology, it's his music that illuminates the brilliance of his legacy. While many can empathize, to some degree, with Jaco when he was at his worst, few if any can compare with him when he was at his best. It is precisely *this* aspect of his legacy that deserves our undivided attention, not the sordid details of a man suffering from illness.

There is a tremendous body of work that Jaco left us that has yet to be thoroughly disseminated. Despite the worldwide availability of his recordings, there is much more to learn about his compositional development as well as his stylistic development as a collaborator—as both sideman and arranger. Hopefully now, more and more of Jaco's work will begin to surface and become available for study, so that we can further understand the tremendous gift he left us and pass it on to the next generation of bassists, composers, and humanity.

ABOUT THE AUTHOR

Sean Malone is a bassist and composer who has performed and recorded with musicians such as Bill Bruford, Steve Hackett, Trey Gunn, Steve Morse, Mike Portnoy, Reeves Gabrels, John Myung, and Mike Keneally. Sean has appeared on over 50 recordings and has performed throughout Europe and North America. His latest CD, *Gordian Knot – Emergent*, is available worldwide from The Laser's Edge (www.lasercd.com). Sean's website can be found at www.seanmalone.net.

In addition, Sean has a Ph.D. in Music Theory from the University of Oregon, where his research interests included music cognition, absolute pitch, and Schenkerian Analysis. He has published and presented his research on the late Canadian pianist Glenn Gould at music theory conferences in Canada and the U.S. Sean is also the author of the *Dictionary of Bass Grooves* (Hal Leonard).

SELECT DISCOGRAPHY:

Sean Malone	*Cortlandt*	AudioImage Records
Sean Malone	*Gordian Knot*	Sensory
Sean Malone	*Gordian Knot – Emergent*	Sensory
Cynic	*Focus*	RoadRunner Records
Various Artists	*Working Man – A Tribute to Rush*	Magna Carta Records
Various Artists	*Guitars That Rule the World vol. 2*	Metal Blade Records
Various Artists	*BassTalk vol. 5*	Hotwire Records

ACKNOWLEDGMENT

Thanks to: Everyone at Hal Leonard, Yoko Miyama for the patience, Carl Woideck for the facts, Ampeg, DR Strings, and Steve Hoek at Serato Software for use of their plug-in for ProTools® "Pitch 'n Time" (www.serato.com).

Bass Notation Legend

Bass music can be notated two different ways: on a *musical staff*, and in *tablature*.

THE MUSICAL STAFF shows pitches and rhythms and is divided by bar lines into measures. Pitches are named after the first seven letters of the alphabet.

TABLATURE graphically represents the bass fingerboard. Each horizontal line represents a string, and each number represents a fret.

3rd string, open   2nd string, 2nd fret   1st & 2nd strings open, played together

HAMMER-ON: Strike the first (lower) note with one finger, then sound the higher note (on the same string) with another finger by fretting it without picking.

PULL-OFF: Place both fingers on the notes to be sounded. Strike the first note and without picking, pull the finger off to sound the second (lower) note.

LEGATO SLIDE: Strike the first note and then slide the same fret-hand finger up or down to the second note. The second note is not struck.

SHIFT SLIDE: Same as legato slide, except the second note is struck.

TRILL: Very rapidly alternate between the notes indicated by continuously hammering on and pulling off.

TREMOLO PICKING: The note is picked as rapidly and continuously as possible.

VIBRATO: The string is vibrated by rapidly bending and releasing the note with the fretting hand.

SHAKE: Using one finger, rapidly alternate between two notes on one string by sliding either a half-step above or below.

NATURAL HARMONIC: Strike the note while the fret hand lightly touches the string directly over the fret indicated.

MUFFLED STRINGS: A percussive sound is produced by laying the fret hand across the string(s) without depressing them and striking them with the pick hand.

BEND: Strike the note and bend up the interval shown.

BEND AND RELEASE: Strike the note and bend up as indicated, then release back to the original note. Only the first note is struck.

RIGHT-HAND TAP: Hammer ("tap") the fret indicated with the "pick-hand" index or middle finger and pull off to the note fretted by the fret hand.

LEFT-HAND TAP: Hammer ("tap") the fret indicated with the "fret-hand" index or middle finger.

SLAP: Strike ("slap") string with right-hand thumb.

POP: Snap ("pop") string with right-hand index or middle finger.

Additional Musical Definitions

- Accentuate note (play it louder)

(accent)

- Accentuate note with great intensity

(staccato)

- Play the note short

⊓ • Downstroke

∨ • Upstroke

D.S. al Coda • Go back to the sign (%), then play until the measure marked "***To Coda***," then skip to the section labelled "**Coda**."

D.C. al Fine • Go back to the beginning of the song and play until the measure marked "***Fine***" (end).

Bass Fig. • Label used to recall a recurring pattern.

Fill • Label used to identify a brief pattern which is to be inserted into the arrangement.

tacet • Instrument is silent (drops out).

- Repeat measures between signs.

- When a repeated section has different endings, play the first ending only the first time and the second ending only the second time.

NOTE: Tablature numbers in parentheses mean:
1. The note is being sustained over a system (note in standard notation is tied), or
2. The note is sustained, but a new articulation (such as a hammer-on, pull-off, slide or vibrato begins), or
3. The note is a barely audible "ghost" note (note in standard notation is also in parentheses).